The Marshall Cavendish
Library of Science Projects

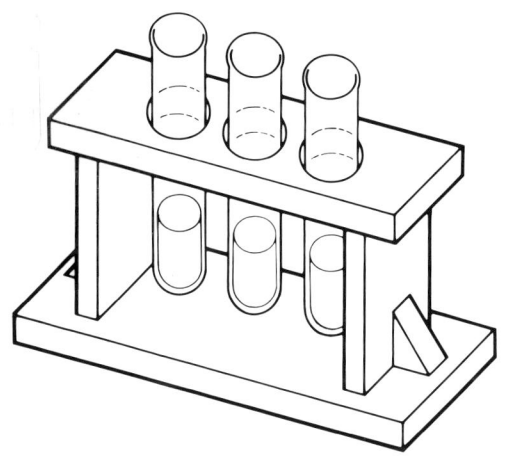

Marshall Cavendish Corporation
London • New York • Toronto

The Marshall Cavendish
SCIENCE PROJECT BOOK
of
MECHANICS

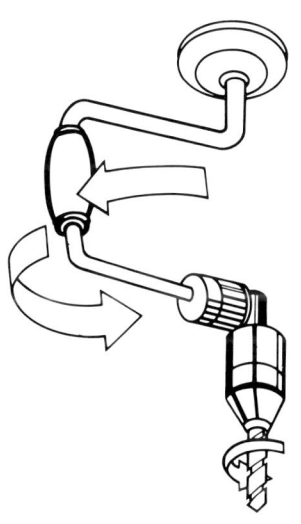

Written by Steve Parker
Illustrated by David Parr

Reference edition published by:
   Marshall Cavendish Corporation
   2415 Jerusalem Avenue
   North Bellmore
   New York 11710

Reference Edition published 1993

The Marshall Cavendish Library of Science Projects
Mechanics

© Marshall Cavendish Limited MCMLXXXVI
© Templar Publishing Limited MCMLXXXV
Illustrations © Templar Publishing Limited MCMLXXXV

All rights reserved. No part of this book may be reproduced or utilized in any form by any means electronic or mechanical including photocopying, recording, or by information storage and retrieval system, without permission from the copyright holder.

Printed and bound in Italy
by L.E.G.O. s.p.a. Vicenza

Library of Congress Cataloguing in Publication Data

Parker, Steve.
   The Marshall Cavendish science project book of mechanics / written by Steve Parker; illustrated by David Parr.—Reference ed.—London; New York: Marshall Cavendish Corp., 1986.
   48 p.: col. ill.; 24 cm.—(The Marshall Cavendish library of science projects; v. 3)
   Includes index.
   Summary: Instructions for a variety of projects and experiments that examine different kinds of machines and how they work.
   ISBN 0-86307-625-4. — ISBN 0-86307-624-6 (set) : $59.70
   1. Mechanics—Juvenile literature. 2. Mechanics—Experiments—Juvenile literature. [1. Mechanics—Experiments. 2. Machinery. 3. Experiments] I. Parr, David, ill. II. Title. III. Series: Parker, Steve. Marshall Cavendish library of science projects; v. 3.
QC127.4.P37 1986   531—dc19   87-404304
                              AACR 2 MARC

Library of Congress   [9001]   AC

PICTURE CREDITS
Pages 6-7: Ford Photographs
Pages 10-11: Ford Photographs
Pages 12-13: Science Photo Library/A. Hart-Davies *(Windmill & power station);* Science Photo Library/Richard Folwell *(Oil platform)*
Pages 18-19: Science Photo Library/Graham Evans; *tr* British Tourist Authrity; *mr* British Leyland; *br* Science Photo Library/NASA
Pages 26-27: Thorn EMI; *tl* British Telecom; *bl* Casio Electronics Ltd; *br* Sony Ltd
Pages 32-33: British Tourist Authority; *tl* British Tourist Authority; *br* Ford Photographs
Pages 38-39: Courtesy of JCB; *tr* British Tourist Authority

CONTENTS

Golden rules	4
Master or servant?	6
Back to basics	8
Laws of motion	10
The force is with you	12
Dream machines	14
Experiments	16
The old and the new	18
The first machines	20
Power for the people	22
Experiments	24
Machine crazy?	26
Mechanics at home	28
Projects	30
On the move	32
Engine power	34
Experiments	36
Field & factory	38
Work horses	40
Things to remember	42

Science is all about discovering more about your world, finding out why certain things happen and how we can use them to help us in our everday lives. SCIENCE PROJECTS looks at all these things. It's packed with exciting experiments and projects for you to do, and fascinating facts for you to remember. It will teach you more about the world around you and to understand how it works.

GOLDEN RULES

This book contains lots of scientific facts and experiments to help you find out more about machines and how they work. Whenever you try one of the experiments, make sure you read all about it before you start. You'll find a list of all the things you need, a step-by-step account of what to do, and finally an explanation of why and how your experiment works.

▶ Always watch what happens very carefully when you're doing an experiment and, if you find it doesn't work the first time, *don't* give up. Consider what could have gone wrong. Are the conditions right? Perhaps the temperature of the room or a draft could have affected your results. Read through the experiment once more, check that everything is just right, and then try, try again. Real scientists may have to do an experiment several times before getting a worthwhile result.

▶ Because you will be such an active scientist, it's a good idea to start collecting for your laboratory. Nearly everything you need for the experiments can be found around your home. For example, bottles and jars will often be used, so when you

GOOD SCIENTISTS...

ALWAYS THINK SAFETY FIRST

Famous scientists take precautions to avoid danger, so that they live to see their results and enjoy their fame. In any project or experiment, especially one you have thought up yourself, consider what it is you are trying to prove and have a good idea of what should happen. Don't do any experiment without planning it 'just see what happens'.

ALWAYS KEEP A NOTEBOOK

Whenever you are involved in scientific activity, keep your *Science Notebook* by your side and fill it with notes and sketches as you go along. Get into the habit of writing up your experiments and observations – your notes will come in handy in the future.

ALWAYS FOLLOW GOOD ADVICE

Advice and instructions, like the leaflets that come with pieces of equipment, should be read and understood. They are there for your safety and help. Good scientists think for themselves, but they are also wise and listen to what others have to say.

see your parents throwing away useful containers, offer to wash them, and then add them to your collection. General things like pens, paper, a ruler, spoons for measuring, and a pair of scissors will also come in handy. You'll need a work bench for your experiments with a hard, solid top that can withstand all the cutting, gluing and other necessary steps. It's a good idea for it to be near a sink too. Store your materials in a nearby cupboard or cardboard box.

▶ Always let your parents know what you are doing. Sometimes you'll need their help, especially if you need to use special tools like pliers or metal cutters. And when it comes to special equipment, like the tin plate on page 25, they'll know where to get it. Your parents may help you to build wooden stands or nail things down when needed. And if you need to use matches or cut things out, always ask their permission first.

▶ Good scientists always clean up when they have finished! After you have done your experiments, throw away anything you won't need again and clean everything else, ready for the next experiment.

NEVER MESS WITH ELECTRICITY

Don't play with electricity or electrical outlets. Carry out all your electrical experiments with low-power batteries (preferably 3 or 4½ volts). Remember, electricity can kill you.

NEVER PLAY WITH CHEMICALS

Avoid mixing chemicals and powders unless you are sure that you know what is going to happen, and always use small quantities. Dangerous chemical mixtures can explode or start a fire or burn your eyes and skin. Make sure any chemicals you keep are properly stored in jars and are correctly labeled.

NEVER FOOL WITH HIGH-PRESSURE EQUIPMENT

Do not play around with gas or liquids under pressure, especially in containers like aerosol cans – even if they seem empty. They can blow up in your face. Dispose of empty aerosols carefully and *never* put them in or near the fire.

MASTER OR SERVANT?

Ask yourself the following question: "How can I lift a car with only one hand?" Your answer might be: "By using a simple machine – a car jack, worked by hand." Then ask yourself another question: "How could I get oil from under the sea bed?" This time the answer might be: "By using a complicated machine – an oil rig, driven by huge diesel and electric engines."

You could also ask yourself a third question: "What exactly is a machine?" Well, the two answers above should give you some clues. First of all, a machine is something that makes work easier. It does a job that we would find difficult or impossible to do on our own. Second, machines usually involve movement. The word 'machinery' probably makes you think of moving parts such as gears, levers, and pistons. Yet there are some machines that are so simple, we don't even think of them as 'machines'. You can read about some of these on page 8.

Basically, machines are there to help us. And they usually have moving parts that combine together to perform a task. But how do they actually work?

First, every machine needs some sort of force to drive it. The force might come from your muscles, as when you struggle to cut the grass with a push-mower. Or it might come from exploding gasoline fumes, as when you stroll lazily across the lawn behind a gasoline mower. The force might also come from electricity, as when you mow the lawn with an electric mower while the orange cord trails behind you! Even if you were to cut the grass with scissors, you would still be using a machine, even though it would be a very simple one worked by your fingers.

Today, it's hard to imagine life without machines. Without them, we would have to build highways by scraping at the earth with our bare hands and carrying it away in buckets

Robots in a modern car factory help to speed up the production line. Once programmed to do its job, the robot makes few other demands of its masters.

on our shoulders. In any case, there wouldn't be much point in making a highway because there would be no cars or trucks to run on it. In fact, the highway workers would probably be late for work anyway because there would be no simple machine to ring its alarm each morning and wake them up on time!

We live in the age of machines. We like to think of them as our servants but, if we wish to continue living in the same easy way that we do now, in some ways machines are also our masters.

BACK TO BASICS

Some machines you come across may seem terribly complicated, while others look relatively simple. But, in fact, all machines are based on a few very straightforward principles. If you asked a good mechanic or engineer to tell you about a complicated machine like a combine harvester, he would be able to explain with ease how each part works. That's partly because he would know all about the simple machines on this page. (In the pictures below, L = Load, E = Effort.)

Lever
A lever is a rigid bar or pole that pivots at a point called the fulcrum. Move one end of the lever down and the other end moves up. If the fulcrum is positioned nearer to one end of the pole than the other, you can use it to lift a heavy weight. The amount you can lift (or, in other words, the force produced) will depend on the distance between the fulcrum and the ends of the lever. One other important thing to remember about the lever, and about many simple machines, is that you won't be able to move a heavy weight very far because what you gain in lifting force, you lose in movement. The Greek mathematician Archimedes once said that if he had a lever long enough and somewhere to pivot it, he could move the whole world! Crowbars, nutcrackers, see-saws and shovels are all types of lever.

Inclined plane
This is like a ramp, slope or hill. It is easier to move a heavy weight up a gentle slope than it is to lift it straight up. It's the same principle as when you find it easier to walk to and fro in zig-zags to climb a hillside, instead of walking up the steepest part.

Wedge
This is made from two inclined planes joined back-to-back. Using only a small amount of force you can push a wedge into a gap and separate two things. A blade is a wedge. The sharper the wedge, the easier it is to cut something, but you do not force the pieces apart so far. You can see the principle of the wedge at work in a pneumatic drill or an ax.

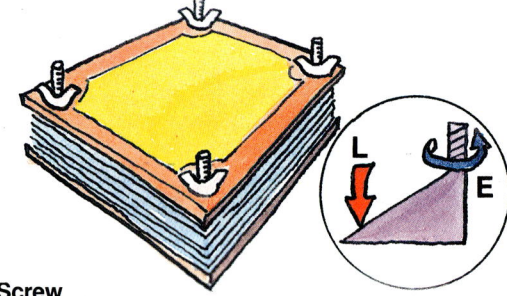

Screw
A screw is an inclined plane wrapped in spiral fashion around a central rod or axle. Screws can be used to lift, press or force things apart. They are extremely useful – some car jacks use the screw principle, as do presses and slicing machines. (Archimedes, who wanted to move the world with his lever, was possibly the inventor of the screw and he lived over 2,000 years ago!)

Pulley
A pulley is another kind of lever. Two or three pulleys linked together will allow you to lift a heavy load quite easily, but once again you won't be able to move it very far. A pulley also changes the direction of movement: you can use it to lift things *up* by pulling *down* on the pulley. And since it's harder to push up than pull down, this makes things less of a chore. You can see pulleys at work in cranes and on some clotheslines.

Wheel and axle
The wheel is a very important but simple machine. It is also a kind of lever, but instead of having a fulcrum it has an axle. Wheels can be used to move things along, such as carts, by reducing the effort needed to move a load about. But they can also be used in lots of other ways – in our drawing, a little effort put into turning the handle of the winch (wheel) will lift a heavy car up the ramps.

Science in action

Something for nothing?
One guiding principle in all machines is that you do not get something for nothing! Suppose you wanted to lift a stone weighing 110 lbs (50 kg) into a cart 3ft 3in (about 100 cms) high. If you were strong you might be able to lift it straight in, but a machine would make the job much easier. If you set up several pulleys, like the ones used on cranes and hoists (see page 21), you would be able to pull the rope and lift the stone into the cart quite easily.

But wait a minute. Both ways of lifting the stone – either straight in, or hoisting it with ropes and pulleys – mean moving the stone the same distance. This means that there is the same amount of work to do in each case.

True, the ropes and pulleys make the job much easier. But you will find that, even with a long pull on the rope, the stone only moves up a small

distance. You will have to pull, and pull, and pull, getting through yards of rope before the stone is high enough to swing over into the skip. Each pull is easy, but there are lots of them! Using the machines is easier, but slower. In the end, both ways add up to the same thing. In science, you *don't* get something for nothing!

LAWS OF MOTION

Have you ever watched a big machine working, such as a tractor engine, and noticed how precisely all the moving parts work together? The engineers who built it calculated all the pressures, forces, weights and measures so that all the parts work together smoothly to produce enormous power just where it's needed.

Obeying the laws

To design a complicated machine you first need to know about the laws governing movement. Isaac Newton was the first to study movement in depth. And he came up with three basic 'laws of motion' that allow us to work out how moving things behave.

Law 1
The first law is that any moving object will carry on moving at the same speed and in the same direction unless a force acts on it to change its speed or direction. For example, if you throw a stone into the air it won't keep going up forever. Two forces – the pull of gravity and resistance from the air – will slow it down, stop it and drag it back to Earth.

Law 2
Any object slows down or speeds up in proportion to the size of the force acting upon it. Also, any change of direction of the movement of the object will be in the same direction as that of the acting force. For example, the stone will fall back to earth at an ever increasing speed since gravity keeps pulling it towards the ground, making it accelerate downwards.

Law 3
For any action, there is an equal and opposite reaction. So when the stone lands, the action of it being stopped by the earth has an opposite reaction – some of the soil will be squashed to leave a small dent.

All this may seem fairly obvious to us nowadays, but in Newton's time people were only just beginning to understand machines and the principles of movement.

All the parts of this car engine have been designed to work together smoothly to provide a turning force at the wheels.

Science in action

Up, down, round and round

There are three main types of movement. The first is *linear* movement, when things go in a straight line. The second is *rotary* movement, when things go round and round. And the third is *oscillating* movement, when things go to-and-fro, back and forth, up and down. Machine parts usually move in one of these ways, or sometimes in a combination of two ways to enable a change from one type of movement to another.

Science discovery

Newton gets a bump on the head

Sir Isaac Newton (1642-1727) is one of the most famous scientists who ever lived. And when you look at his list of achievements it's easy to see why. Besides studying motion and working out the three laws, he invented systems of mechanics and mathematics to deal with moving objects. He invented a special type of telescope (called, as you might expect, the *Newtonian* telescope). And he also formulated Newton's law of cooling, which has given us a way to work out how fast an object loses heat. But of all the things he did during his life, Isaac Newton is best remembered for one thing: he was the first man to realize that gravity is a force just like any other.

Gravity is a force which pulls things down toward the centre of the earth. Like other forces, it can be measured and must be taken into account when designing machinery.

There's a simple tale (which you may have already heard) about how Newton came to understand gravity. The story goes that he was sitting under an apple tree. Suddenly, an apple dropped from the tree and landed on his head.. and the nature of gravity became clear to him!

Because of Newton's achievements, a measure of force has been named after him. A *Newton* is the amount of force needed to give an object weighing 2.2 lbs (one kilogram) an acceleration of 3.28 ft (one meter) per second every second.

A diesel train whizzing along a track is a good example of all three movements. Linear movement is shown in the train traveling forward along the track. Rotary movement can be seen in the wheels turning. And, inside the engine, there is oscillating movement as the piston moves to and fro within the cylinder.

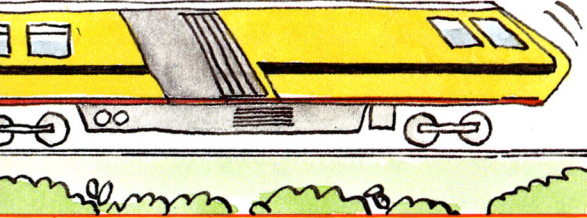

THE FORCE IS WITH YOU

All machines need energy to make them work. In ancient times it came from the muscles of peasants and animals, like horses and oxen. (In fact, in medieval times squirrels were even added to the workforce! They were put in little treadmill

wheels which were linked up to turn small machines!) What's more, throughout history man has used the earth's natural elements, like wind and water, to provide energy for his machines. Then, during the Industrial Revolution of the late eighteenth and early nineteenth centuries, steam power was introduced and it changed the world.

From the early days, man has sought and found new sources of energy. Earlier in this century the internal combustion engine, based on gasoline power, began to take over. Then even more recently came atomic power. Nowadays, we get energy from all sorts of places – from the coal and natural gas stored deep in the earth, to the sun which beats down on us every day.

Which word is which?

You will come across the words energy, force, power and work many times in this book. They are all closely related to the subject of mechanics but each word means something quite different:
Energy is the capacity or ability to do work. If you are tired, you don't have the *energy* to move. And if a car runs out of gas its engine won't have the *energy* to run. Both a machine's and your own energy is measured in joules.
Force is the 'push' that makes an object move, or change its speed or direction. It is measured in Newtons.
Work is simply explained as the result of a force! When you open a door, the force of your muscles makes it open, and the open door is the *work* done. Work is measured in joules, like energy.
Power is the rate at which work is done. Take the work done by a machine and divide it by the length of time it took to do, and you will find its *power*. It is measured in horsepower or watts.

You can see how closely these words are interconnected. To help you remember (and understand!) the meaning of all four words, here's a simple story.

1 *Your parents offer to take you to school in the car. The gas in the tank contains* energy, *in the form of chemical bonds in the molecules of gasoline.*

2 *The bonds explode in the engine to produce a* force *that pushes the pistons down and, with the help of gears and wheels, makes the car travel along the road.*

All these things supply us with energy which we can put to work in lots of different ways.

However, with such a large number of machines – and people – in our world, priorities are changing. Instead of thinking about which type of energy is

easiest to obtain, or which type of machine is easiest to build, we must start planning ahead. We must use sources of energy carefully so that they do not run out. And we must also use them thoughtfully so that the machines that depend on them do not pollute our world.

3 The work is done by moving you, your parents and the car from your house to the school gates. More work will be done in moving everybody back!

4 You can work out the power of the car engine by dividing the amount of work done by the time it took for you to get to school. (To find out the maximum power you car is capable of, you'd have to test it on a special rig.)

Science factfile

But is it efficient?

To design and build a machine you have to consider whether it is going to be 'efficient'. After all, no one wants a machine that overheats, makes a lot of noise, or wastes fuel! So the general idea is to make every machine as efficient as possible.

'Efficiency' is simply the amount of energy (as work) produced by the machine, divided by the amount of energy put into the machine (as fuel). The answer is usually written as a percentage. You can see below how our efficiency level compares with some of today's machines.

▶ A car engine is about 25 to 30% efficient.
▶ An electric motor is 80 to 90% efficient.
▶ You are about 25% efficient!

The two types of energy

Electricity, wind, heat, light, water, and solar power (light and heat from the sun) are all forms of energy that man uses to make his machines work. The chemical energy that man has discovered in coal, oil, and natural gas is also used. But all these different sources of energy can be explained in two simple terms – kinetic and potential.

Kinetic energy is any energy that comes from movement. The wind's energy is kinetic and can be harnessed to do work by the sails of a windmill or the body of a kite.

Potential energy is the energy of which any object is capable because of its position. For example, a coiled spring has potential energy to release and so does a cart sitting at the top of a hill. Once potential energy is released, however, it immediately becomes kinetic.

A good example of both kinetic and potential energy at work is a swinging pendulum. At the extreme end of its swing, the pendulum possesses potential energy. But, when it is actually in the process of swinging, the pendulum's energy is kinetic.

DREAM MACHINES

Inventors through the ages have often dreamed of making a machine that just continued working all by itself forever, and ever, and ever. Once started, such a machine would work on its own with no need for fuel or any other energy source. It would cost nothing to run and might even provide a free source of power. It would certainly make the inventor very rich. But no one has ever built a so-called perpetual motion machine – because it is an impossible task.

Before about 1850 there was no scientific reason to stop people from thinking that such machines were possible. Then the scientist Hermann von Helmholtz came up with the *First Law of Thermodynamics*. This law says that energy cannot be created or destroyed. It can only be changed from one form to another, such as from electricity to light or from chemicals to heat. So, from this, it followed that a perpetual motion machine, which had no energy going in but lots of energy coming out, was an impossible idea. Once again, as Helmholtz pointed out, you cannot get something for nothing!

The problem of friction

The main enemy of perpetual motion is friction. The problem is that friction 'steals' energy (the energy of movement) and turns it into other forms of energy – mostly heat. All scientists and engineers try to

Science in action

Fighting friction

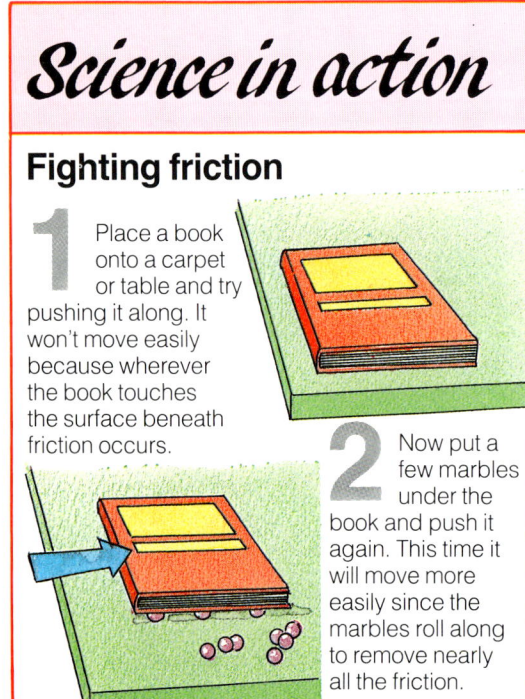

1 Place a book onto a carpet or table and try pushing it along. It won't move easily because wherever the book touches the surface beneath friction occurs.

2 Now put a few marbles under the book and push it again. This time it will move more easily since the marbles roll along to remove nearly all the friction.

prevent friction in the machines they design and build so energy isn't wasted by overheating. But you can never get rid of friction altogether – which is one reason why most big machines get hot and also why they eventually wear out.

So how is it that friction prevents perpetual motion machines from working? Suppose you spin a heavy flywheel that turns on well-oiled bearings. The flywheel may go round for hours and hours but eventually it will stop. This is because, as the wheel turns, it 'slides' past molecules of air, and when one thing slides past another the result is… friction. Friction makes the air around the wheel warm up and it 'steals' kinetic energy from the wheel. Even if you created a vacuum for the wheel to turn in it would still stop eventually, due to friction in the bearings.

But although friction can be a nuisance when you're designing a machine or trying to make something go faster or for longer, we couldn't do without it. If there was no friction, we would slip backwards every time we tried to walk forwards! What's more, boy scouts could not make a fire by rubbing two sticks together and a violin string would make no sound when stroked by its bow.

Overcoming friction

But to the engineer and mechanic, friction poses two problems. First is loss of energy. For example, about one-fifth of a car engine's power is used to overcome the friction between its moving parts. Greater still is the problem of wear and tear. Modern machines usually have enough power to compensate for energy lost through friction, and if any of their parts get too hot they can be cooled down. But when a part wears away or breaks, this causes much more trouble. To try and overcome this problem, modern lubricants like oil and grease have been designed to reduce the friction in order to reduce the wear. That's why car engines occasionally need topping up with oil and the chain on your bicycle needs greasing every now and then.

Many hundreds of years ago, the great artist and inventor Leonardo da Vinci designed this perpetual motion machine. The bulbs on the end of its arms were partly filled with mercury and, as their weight shifted, would cause the wheel to turn – forever! Leonardo soon came to realize though, that all such machines were doomed to failure.

Science factfile

A mouse in the machine

One of the oddest ideas for a perpetual motion machine was based on 'mouse power'. The theory was that a group of mice could live in a sealed glass container along with some plants. The mice could eat the plants; the plants could grow using the droppings of the mice as fertilizer. Water given off by the mice, in their breath, and by the plants' leaves could be collected by a condenser unit and recycled. The mice would breathe the oxygen produced by the plant process of photosynthesis; the carbon dioxide needed by the plants for photosynthesis would be breathed out by the mice.

The sealed cage would be a self-contained and self-perpetuating ecosystem. Here, surely, was a real perpetual motion machine. Except for one small problem: plants need the energy in sunlight in order to grow. So when the sun fades away, the machine stops…

EXPERIMENT · EXPERI

There is a fascinating toy named after the famous scientist Sir Isaac Newton (who you can read about on page 11). It's called a *Newton's Cradle* and you can use it to show how energy can be passed from one object to another.

Newton's Cradle

To make your own Newton's Cradle you will need four plastic bottles (like the sort used for liquid soap), two pencils, five large and five small glass beads, some scissors, a pen-knife and a reel of strong cotton thread.

step 2

Now cut five 16 inch (40 cm) lengths of thread. Thread one of the small beads onto each length and slide it along until it reaches halfway. Next, thread both ends of one piece of thread through one of the large beads. Slide it down until it is sitting above the smaller bead, as in the picture. Then tie a simple knot in the thread and pull it tight so it keeps the beads in place. You may need to tie several knots like this to make the beads secure. Make a note of how many knots you've tied, then repeat the whole procedure for the rest of the beads.

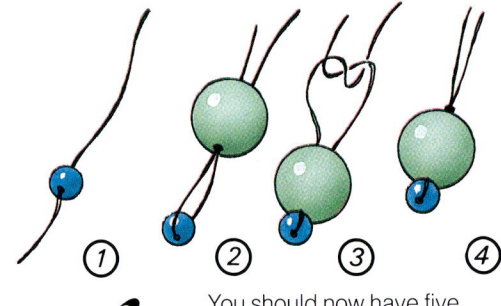

step 3

You should now have five lengths of thread with glass beads secured at their middles. Your next step is to make notches in the pencil for the threads to rest in. This will stop the beads from sliding about and moving apart. Tie one end of each piece of thread to one of the pencils. Space them out so the beads are hanging side by side and just touching. Then make a notch for each thread.

step 1

Cut the tops off the plastic bottles (having first made sure that they are quite empty!) so that they are all 8 in (20 cms) high. Then cut a small wedge in the top of each one to support the ends of the pencils, as shown below. To keep the bottles from moving around you could put something heavy inside them – a handful of marbles for instance.

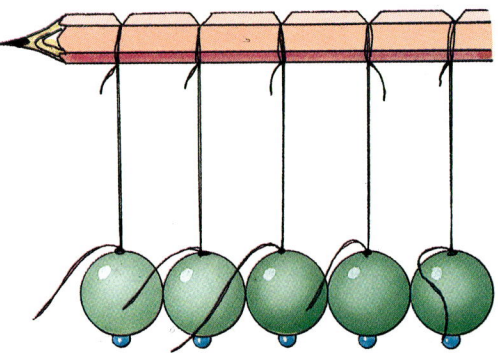

EMENT · EXPERIMENT

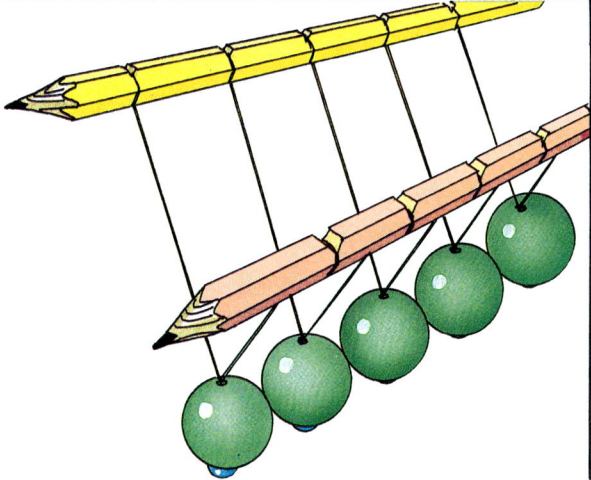

Step 4

Now lay your second pencil next to the first and mark off the position of the notches. It is important that the notches on both pencils should be in exactly the same place, so take care! If the beads should end up hanging with the thread at different angles on either side, then it could affect the end result of your Cradle. Tie the free ends of thread to the second pencil so that the beads hang together in a tidy row.

Support the pencils by sliding them into the ready-made wedges on the bottles.

Step 5

Before you set your Newton's Cradle in motion, do a final check to see that all the beads are hanging side by side and just touching one another. You may need to make some adjustments before the Cradle is ready for action!

Once you're sure everything is just right, try lifting up the first bead in the row and letting it swing back to hit the others. What happens? Now try it with the first two… and three… You can see that when the first bead swings back and hits the remaining four, the last bead in the row swings out. This is because the energy from the movement of the first bead has been transferred from one bead to the next. But it is only the fifth bead that is free to move, using its newly-received energy to swing out and back again. If you don't interfere, this energy will be passed back and forth. Slowly, however, the swing will get smaller and smaller until the beads eventually hang still again.

Can you think of any other toys or games, apart from Newton's Cradle, which illustrate the principles of energy transfer? What about marbles and pocket billiards?

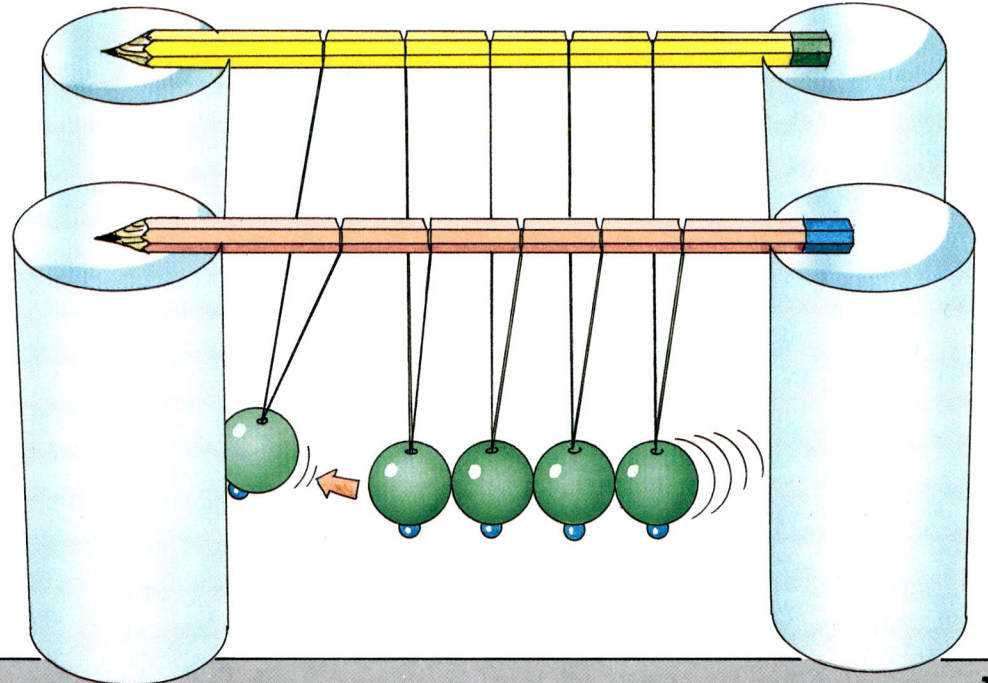

THE OLD AND THE NEW

In ancient times there were very few machines around. And those that did exist were extremely simple. Cartwheels, waterwheels, levers, catapults, ropes, pulleys and screws all helped make things easier. But the main machine of this era was something called a human being. This machine was self-repairing, needed only one meal a day to keep it running, kept itself clean and was capable of doing many different kinds of work. Human beings planted crops and harvested them; they fetched water and made clothes; and they constructed all sorts of buildings, from mud huts to giant pyramids. You could say that this was the age of *People Power*.

Nowadays, we can't move without running into machines. We use dozens of them each day, for everything and anything. There are machines for curling your hair and opening cans; machines for cutting the grass, and planting the crops; and some people even have machines inside their bodies to help them remain healthy. In fact, machines are so important that we even look at history in terms of them...

After many years of people being the main 'machines', things gradually started to change. In the mid-1700's the world moved into the *Mechanical Age*, with the introduction of the steam engine, spinning jenny, weaving loom and cotton gin. Factories sprang up and the Industrial Revolution began (which you can read more about on page 22). Next came the railways and the *Age of Steam,* when locomotives

Progress, progress, progress

▶ In 1830, the first regular British steam passenger train ran. It had a $6^{1}/_{4}$ mile track between Canterbury and Whitstable, Kent. Today, there are 10,541 miles worth of train routes in Britain.

▶ In December 1894 the first British-built car using an internal combustion engine took to the roads. The car, called the Bremer after its creator Frederick William Bremer, had a maximum speed of about 15 mph. Now not even a hundred years later, the fastest cars on the open market reach speeds of 170 mph.

puffed their way through the countryside carrying people and goods. In 1914 thousands of Model T Ford cars rolled off the production line and the *Age of the Car* was here.

In the twentieth century machines have developed so fast that one *Age* is soon replaced by another! In the 1950's

Waterwheels have been around for thousands of years. And unlike some of man's modern inventions, like the train, the car and the rocket, they have remained very simple.

the skies were filled with the roar of engines, and the *Jet Age* began. At the same time, televisions and transistor radios invaded our homes as we entered the *Electronics Age.* By 1957 the *Space Age* had started with the launch of the first spacecraft and, only twelve years later, man was walking on the moon – thanks to the crew of *Apollo 11.*

During the past six or seven years, the *Computer Age* has revolutionized our daily lives. And if you look at our rate of progress so far this century, you can see that the next *Age* is probably just around the corner!

THE FIRST MACHINES

Old machines are fascinating. It is often easier to appreciate them than their modern counterparts, perhaps because they are so simple that you can almost understand how they work by just looking at them! They are usually built out of familiar materials like wood, stone, and iron, and they are all based on the simplest principles of mechanics.

Here are some of the first machines ever invented. Most of them are so old that we don't know who the inventors were. But, nevertheless, many of them are still used today. (In these drawings M = Movement, F = Force.)

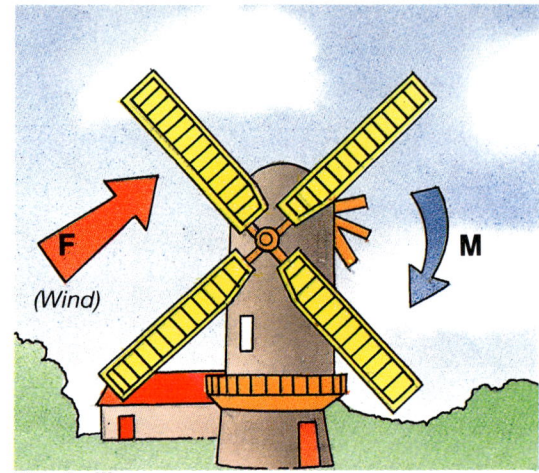

Windmills
Windpower has been used for centuries as a free source of energy. In Asia people were using windmills over two thousand years ago, but the idea didn't catch on in Europe until about 1200. The first windmills were used to pump water from wells and rivers – it was not until later on that man thought of using them to grind corn into flour.

Waterwheels
The waterwheel was invented well before 100 BC, to take advantage of a free energy source – moving water. They were often used to raise water from rivers into aquaducts or gullies. The water was then channeled to flow into towns or used to irrigate the land. And, as with windmills, the waterwheel was later used to turn grinding stones to make flour – which is how the watermill was born.

Plows
The plow must be one of the oldest farming machines in the world. In its simplest form, it was nothing more than a wedge-shaped blade (called a plowshare) that cut into the soil. Early plows were made of wood or stone and dug a simple groove in the ground (called a furrow) in which seeds could be planted. But in AD 100 the design changed so that the plow could also be used to turn over soil. This exposed fresh earth which was much better for the crops planted there. Less than two hundred years ago, the first iron plows were made, but they were still pulled by people, oxen or horses. It wasn't until the early 1900s that the tractor arrived to make plowing the fields an even easier job!

Wheels and rollers

The first rollers were probably nothing more than straight tree trunks with their branches cut off, or suitably shaped boulders. They were used to move heavy objects which were laid across them and pulled along (which is a much easier method of moving something than just trying to drag it along the ground). The idea of the wheel probably came from the roller, since a wheel is really just a very short roller. Early wheels were made by slicing a disc from a tree trunk or by cutting planks of wood into a circular shape. The idea of spoked wheels didn't come along until much later. They were lighter and springier than solid wheels which made them useful for vehicles that carried people, since they made the ride more comfortable.

Block-and-tackle

The block-and-tackle is an arrangement of ropes and pulleys used for lifting and towing, and it too has been around for centuries. In fact, Archimedes (who you can read more about in the panel) is said to have designed a system of pulleys that would allow him to pull a large ship up a slipway and right out of the water – all on his own!

Science in action

The old and the new of Archimedes' screw

Many old machines have new counterparts, and it's interesting to spot old ideas in new machinery.

Archimedes' screw was first used in ancient Egypt to lift water from the River Nile, over its banks and into the dry fields beyond. The screw turned round and round and water flowed in at the bottom, up through the screw thread and out at the top.

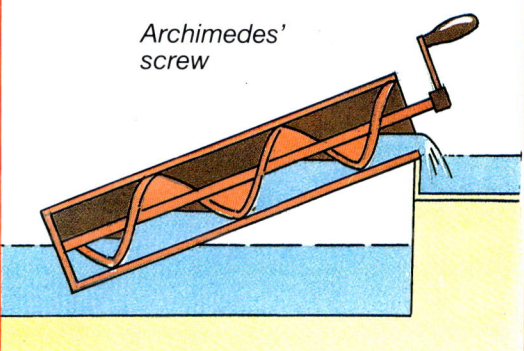

Archimedes' screw

Nowadays, modern garbage trucks use a similar idea – called an 'impeller screw' – to compress all the rubbish they collect. Naturally, the truck's metal screw is a hundred times stronger and more powerful than Archimedes' old wooden version, but the principle is exactly the same.

Can you think of other similarities between old and new machines? Try comparing an ancient waterwheel with a modern hydroelectric dam, or an old windmill with a modern jet turbine engine.

Impeller screw

POWER FOR THE PEOPLE

In 1705, the English inventor Thomas Newcomen built a new and powerful machine. It used the energy locked up in the chemical bonds inside coal. When the coal burned, it gave off heat which was then used to boil water. The boiling water gave off steam. This expanded to provide a pushing force which could move a piston along inside a cylinder. In other words, Newcomen invented the very first steam engine.

Full steam ahead!

In 1765 James Watt designed a much improved version of the original steam engine. Suddenly, a new and powerful way to drive machinery was available. For hundreds of years people had only their own energy and muscles, their animals, and the wind and water to help them. Now machines could be driven by steam engines that could run all day without getting tired. All that was needed was a supply of coal, water, and the occasional overhaul to keep them going.

Quickly the steam engine became incorporated into all kinds of machinery. New machines were invented almost every day – they could make all sorts of things quickly and cheaply, like clothes, glass, furniture, and vehicles, and, of course, more machines! People wanted all the goods that machines could make, and more. It really was the beginning of a revolution – the machines were about to arrive in force!

Industry arrives

Gradually the landscape began to change. Huge buildings called factories were made to house the new machines. People were needed to look after them – to keep them clean, working, and supplied with fuel and raw materials. Towns and cities grew up around the factories as workers left the countryside to work with the machines. The new word was 'industry' and the great changes of

Science discovery

Watt horsepower?

With the Industrial Revolution came the need to measure power. But no one could do so until they had a unit of power to base their calculations on. James Watt solved the problem.

In the eighteenth century, horses were still used for many jobs, so Watt measured how much power one horse could produce. He worked out that the average horse could lift a weight of 550 lbs a distance of 1 foot in 1 second. This he called 'one horsepower' and it quickly became the standard power unit. When scientists changed to metric measurements, the horsepower changed too. Oddly, the metric unit of power is called the watt after the inventor of the old unit! However, car engines are still measured in horsepower.

The car known as the Citroên 2CV is so-called because it has the power of 'deux chevaux' – meaning two horses!

that time came to be known as the *Industrial Revolution*.

The Revolution continued through the late eighteenth and nineteenth centuries, and some of the most important machines which appeared during this time are shown here. However, it eventually became clear that the coal-fired steam engines were an inefficient and dirty way of driving machinery. Towns became clogged with soot and smog, and many of the machines were dangerous to work on. Scientists worked hard to find new sources of power which were cleaner and more efficient so today we have many different ways of powering our machines.

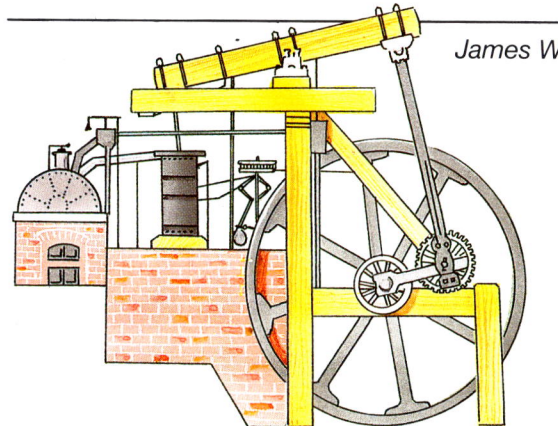

James Watt's steam engine

Moving machines
▶ In the 1770's and 1780's James Watt improved the design of the steam engine so that it became a useful source of power for almost any machine.
▶ In 1804 Richard Trevithick invented a steam engine that ran on wheels along an iron track – the first steam locomotive.
▶ In 1825 George Stephenson started the first public railway. The passengers were pulled by his steam locomotive *Locomotion*.

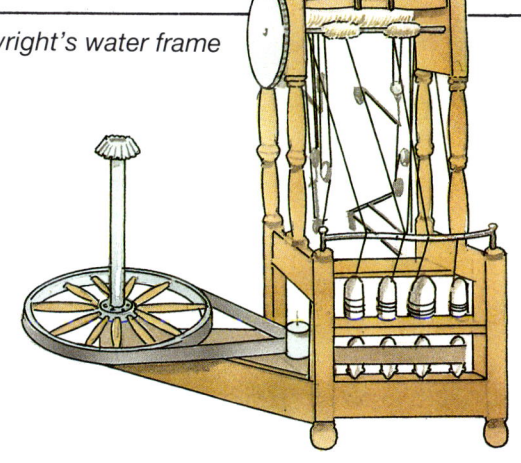

Richard Arkwright's water frame

Spinning machines
▶ In 1764 James Hargreaves' spinning jenny speeded up the production of woollen thread. One jenny had 120 spindles for the thread, compared to the old hand-operated spinning wheel which had only one.
▶ In 1769 Richard Arkwright invented a machine to make cotton thread. Cotton could not be spun easily by hand, but Arkwright's 'water frame' could be used to make good-quality thread. This meant that weaving looms could then make all-cotton cloth.

John Kay's flying shuttle

Weaving machines
▶ In 1733 John Kay invented the flying shuttle, which meant that looms could work at a much faster rate, weaving double the width in half the time.
▶ In 1786 Edmund Cartwright added a steam engine to the basic loom design to make the first power loom.

EXPERIMENT · EXPERI

Before the eighteenth century, man relied heavily on natural sources of energy, like the wind and running water. On this page is a way to use one of the world's earliest energy sources – the sun – to make your own special stove.

The Industrial Revolution, however, brought about enormous changes and some even greater inventions. One of the most significant discoveries of the time was steam, or rather, the force that steam produces. On the opposite page, you can find out how to make a simple steam turbine. Turbines like this were once widely used to provide the power for cotton mills and other industries.

Experiment 2
Supper by sunlight

Most stoves these days run off gas or electricity. But on a clear day you could use the sun's energy to cook yourself a snack! Try it and see. All you need is a large bowl, some baking foil, a lump of clay and a potato (the smaller the better!) Some scissors, tape and a spoon will help too.

Step 1

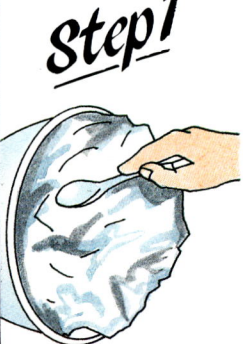

Tear yourself out a sheet of tin foil, big enough to cover the inside of your bowl. (Be careful of the serrated edge on the box.) Put it inside the bowl with the shiny side facing outwards. Then, with the back of a spoon, smooth the surface of the foil down until it looks like a mirror. Stick any spare foil to the outside of the bowl with tape.

Step 2

Stick a lump of clay to the bottom of the bowl. This will now hold your potato in place.

Step 3

Now take your solar stove into the garden. Put it at an angle so that the sun shines directly into the bowl. Leave it for an hour or two, and when you return you should find your meal ready!

The sun's rays will reflect on to the potato, heat it up and, eventually cook it. In hot, tropical countries stoves similar to this, but using concave mirrors, are often used. Today, scientists are keen to find new ways to capture the sun's energy. Solar power stations have been built, and solar panels are used to heat some homes. Have you got solar panels in your home?

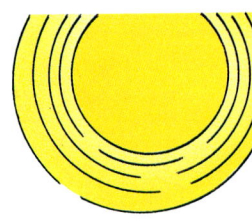

EXPERIMENT · EXPERIMENT

Experiment 3

Making a steam turbine

To make your own steam turbine you will need an empty tin can with a lid, a small sheet of tin plate, a cocktail stick, heat-resistant glue, a pair of scissors, some pliers, a hammer and a nail, a ruler, a pair of compasses, and a pencil. You will also need some water and the use of a bunsen burner or hotplate.

Step 1

Cut out a circle of tin plate (about $2^{3}/_{8}$ in [6 cms] in diameter) and divide it into twelve sections as shown. Cut along each line, stopping roughly $3/_{8}$ in (1 cm) short of the center. Then pierce a hole in the center using your hammer and nail, just big enough for your cocktail stick.

Step 2

Put the wheel onto the cocktail stick and glue it in a central position. Leave it somewhere safe while it dries. Once the glue is set, bend each section of your tin plate wheel round as shown, using the pliers. You have now finished making a *rotor*: the individual sections on it are called *blades*.

Step 3

Now cut out two strips of tin plate about $2^{3}/_{8}$ in (6 cms) long by $3/_{8}$ in (1 cm) wide. Make a hole about $3/_{8}$ in below the top of one end of each. Then bend the other two ends at right angles to form a bracket. Put your rotor between the brackets and then glue the brackets to the tin lid. Finally, pierce a hole just underneath the blades of the turbine. This will form an 'escape route' for the steam.

Step 4

Now your water turbine is complete! To get it working, first half fill the tin with water and firmly replace the lid. Then position the tin over a bunsen burner or the burner on your parents' stove (with their permission, of course).

As the water beings to boil (and consequently expands), steam will be forced out of the hole. And the rising force of the steam will start your rotor spinning. In large turbines this movement is captured to power generators or machinery. Remember, let your turbine cool before moving it.

MACHINE MAD?

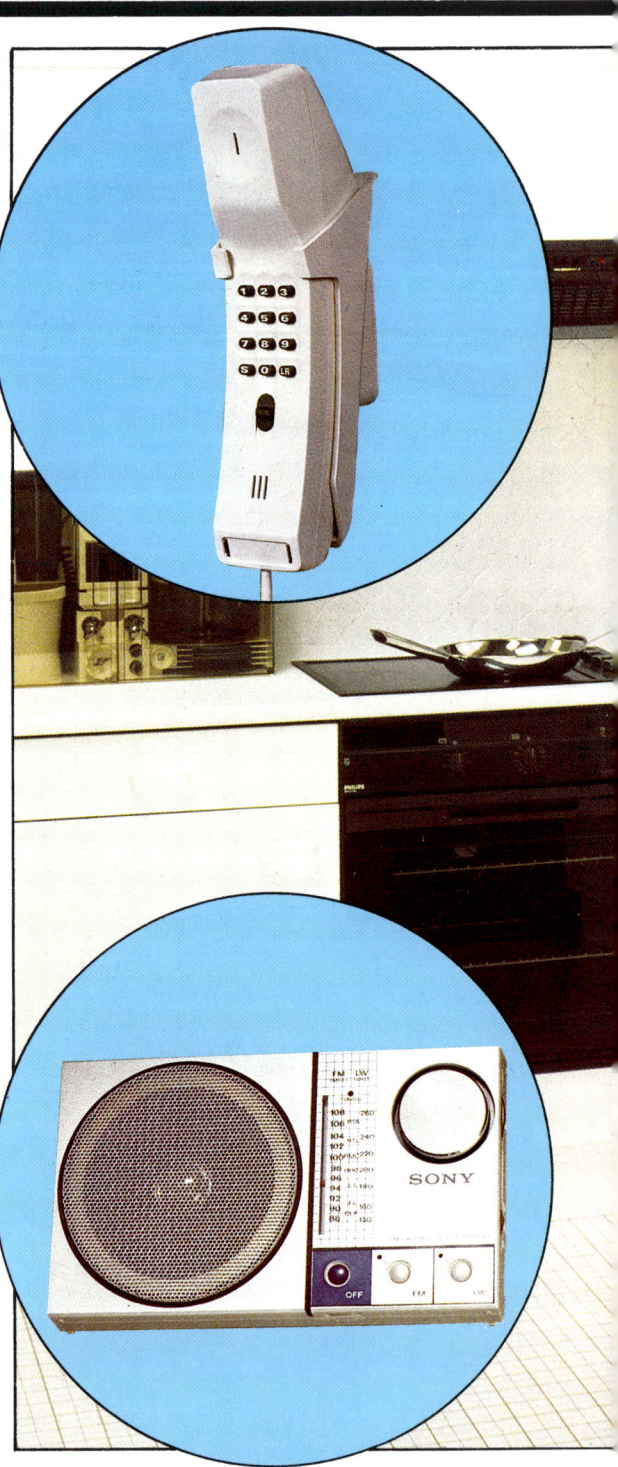

First thing in the morning a machine makes a noise to wake you up. You go downstairs to have breakfast and a machine makes your toast. A machine keeps the milk cold that you put on your cereal. A machine heats the water for your cup of coffee. A machine tells you the weather forecast for the day ahead. You might even use a machine to brush your teeth! Your home is full of machines.

Most houses have lots of tools, machines and gadgets designed to make our lives easier: They are 'labor saving'. Only a few dozen years ago all housework was done by hand and most of the day was spent cleaning, washing, and doing other boring and tiring chores. Now, most households have a washing machine, a sewing machine, a fridge, a vacuum cleaner, and a mixer or blender to help with the chores. Some even have a dishwasher, a freezer, a microwave oven, and an electric polisher!

Many of these machines are powered by electricity. Houses built 75 years ago had only a few electric sockets, sometimes just one in the kitchen and one in the living room. But nowadays there are sockets in virtually every room – because virtually every room has machines that need plugging in.

Machines save us time and energy round the house. So, what do we do with all this extra time? You might be able to guess when you hear people say that they 'can't live' without their video recorder or home computer. We easily fill our spare time – by playing with more machines!

The machine-age kitchen is designed to make your life easier and give you more time – time to enjoy yourself with other machines!

MECHANICS AT HOME

Many machines around the house are ingeniously simple. They use the basic principles of mechanics, explained on pages 8 and 9. But no matter how simple a machine is, someone had to invent it. Several people have made their fortunes by inventing simple machines that soon became indispensable in virtually every household. Take the can opener, for example.

Like many of the machines we use at home every day, the can opener is so elementary that we take it for granted. It uses two basic principles – the lever and the wedge. And like most good ideas, it is simplicity itself. (In fact, the can opener was invented in 1863, 53 years *after* someone had thought of a way of preserving food by sealing it in metal cans! So until the can opener arrived people had to open their canned food with a hammer and chisel!)

The advantage of a simple machine is that it's cheap to make and easy to use. What's more, it has so few moving parts that it hardly ever breaks down.

An electric can opener, on the other hand, may save you time and effort, but it's far more complicated to manufacture and has more moving parts to go wrong. And if there's a power loss, you might have to go without your dinner!

Most households also have a number of complicated machines. We try to take these for granted too, but sometimes it isn't so easy…

"It's been a terrible day: First my alarm clock failed and I overslept. Then the electric stove blew a fuse so I couldn't have my bacon and eggs. I got outside and the car wouldn't start so I had to walk all the way to work. And when I got home at lunchtime the washing machine had leaked water all over the floor. After cleaning that up, I sat down to watch some television and, BANG, the TV set blew up! Keep busy, I said to myself, so I tried to do some vacuuming. But, would you believe it, the drive belt snapped and it started blowing out dust all over the floor. Finally, I had a nice hot bath and washed my hair. But when I tried to dry it, the hairdrier overheated and I had to go to bed with it all wet. What a dreadful day!"

All this goes to show that we rarely notice our machines – that is, until they go wrong. And the more complicated a machine is, the more likely it is to break down. The problem is that we are so dependent on today's machines. For instance, a broken vacuum cleaner is a good excuse for not keeping the house clean. But vacuum cleaners weren't even around before 1910, so for hundreds of years people managed to keep their homes spick and span with just a duster, dustpan and broom.

Nowadays we feel that many domestic machines are essential: what would we do without them? An enormous industry has grown up around making them, selling them, and then servicing them when they go wrong! They have also become status symbols – so some people might buy the latest model toaster even though they can't afford much bread!

Complicated machines

29

PROJECT · PROJECT · PRO

If you take the time to look, you will find lots of machines in your home which use the simple principles explained on pages 8 and 9. Here we have picked on a few examples of common machines that easily demonstrate levers, wedges, screws and other basic machines at work. Can you think of any more? The kitchen and garage are good places to look.

Rotary cheesegrater

A rotary cheesegrater uses three simple machines to do its job.

1 This part of the grater uses the wheel and axle principle. By using a little force on the handle you can create a bigger force at the center (where the cheese touches the wheel).

2 The part of the grater that presses the cheese onto the wheel is really a type of lever. By applying a force to the middle of the lever, you can cause a force at the end where the lever presses on the cheese.

3 All the tiny holes on the grating wheel are really small wedges. Each one cuts into the cheese and slices off thin strips as you turn the handle.

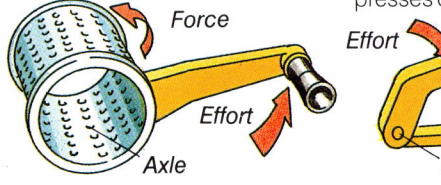
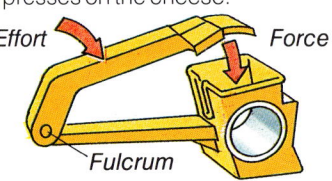
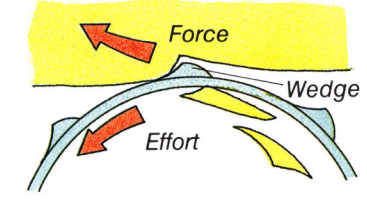

Pliers

The pliers in our drawing use two simple principles to do their job.

The cutting edge is made up of two wedges that can be used to cut metal wire.

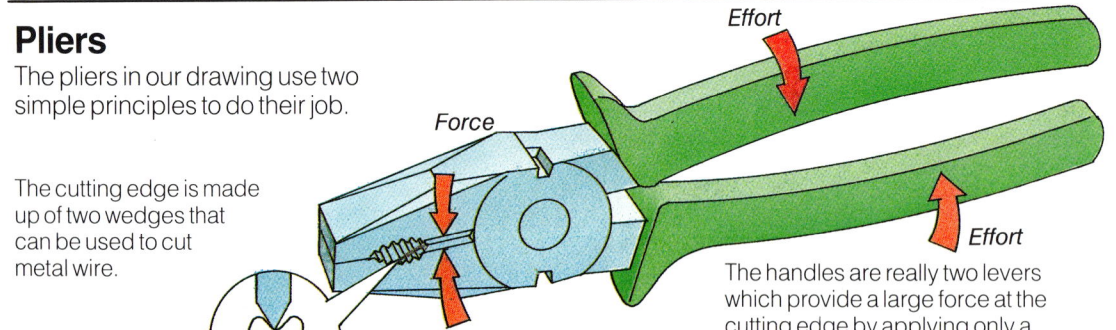

The handles are really two levers which provide a large force at the cutting edge by applying only a little effort at the handles.

JECT · PROJECT · PROJECT

Here are some other machines that you can probably find in your home, together with the basic principles that make them work.

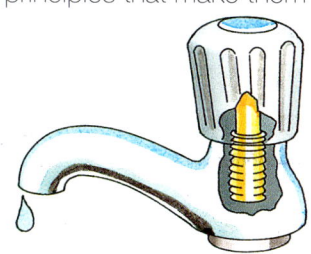

Tap
A tap uses a kind of lever as its handle. This twists a screw inside the tap which allows the water to flow when on, and halts it when off.

Chisel
This chisel uses a wedge as its cutting edge to split wood.

Drills
Drills are used to bore holes in wood. They use two simple principles to work. The first is the wheel and axle, which allows the drill to revolve. And the second is the screw, which is used to drill holes in wood.

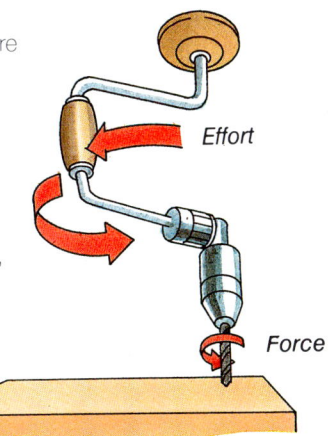

Effort

Force

Grinder
Inside this grinder there is a large screw. Turning the handle provides the force that turns the screw that grinds the meat!

A hundred machines?

If you're reading this at home, stop and look around you. How many machines can you see? If you're in your bedroom you might see an alarm clock or clock/radio, model cars and airplanes, or even some roller skates. Now imagine doing this for every room in the house. How many machines do you think there would be altogether? And which room would have the most? The kitchen or garage usually wins.

Try making a list in your *Science Notebook* of all the different machines in your house. Can you find a hundred? Remember when you're looking around that some machines are made to look good and are put on display – grandfather clocks and stereo systems are examples. Others, like pliers or car grease-guns, are not meant to be seen and are usually hidden away in cupboards or drawers.

When you've finished your list you could try and get your friends to compile ones for their own homes, and compare results.

1. Kettle
2. Can opener
3. Coffee grinder
4. Food mixer
5. Washing machine
6. Cooker
7. Fridge
8. Toaster
9. Stereo
10. Vacuum cleaner
11. Scissors
12. Knife sharpener
13. Ice-cream scoop

ON THE MOVE

In the beginning, man had only his own legs to get him from A to B. Then he discovered that horses and other animals could be trained to carry him from place to place. With the wheel came the cart and the coach, so heavy loads could at last be pulled without too much effort. However, wheels only roll easily on hard, flat ground, so roads had to be built before things could really start moving.

For centuries the best way to travel across land was on horseback or in vehicles pulled by animals. Traveling by water was simpler, though, which was one reason why lots of people lived near rivers, lakes or the sea. Heavy goods could be moved by boat much more easily than they could by horse and cart. In the Middle Ages, great sea ports grew up and sailing ships carried cargo from one country to another.

Then, when the machines of the Industrial Revolution came along, engineers and mechanics were quick to invent new ways to travel. The steam-powered locomotive was one of the first, as you can read on page 22. Later in the 1800s, the steam-powered car was tried but it was too heavy and low-powered to be of much use. Steam-driven boats fared better – the first working 'steamer' was a paddle-wheeled tug that chugged up and down the Forth and Clyde Canal in Scotland from 1801.

For ordinary people, however, the real revolution in transport started at the beginning of the twentieth century. People were already traveling on the

railways, but very few had their own personal method of transport. In 1885 a German named Karl Benz started to change all that by building the first gasoline driven car. And thirty years later

Nowadays we tend to take planes, trains and motor vehicles for granted. Yet they've only been around for a hundred years or so!

Across the Atlantic

▶ In 1498 Christopher Columbus took over three weeks to cross the Atlantic and discover America.

▶ The fastest Atlantic crossing by boat was by the liner *United States* in 1952. She took four days.

▶ In 1919 John Alcock and Arthur Brown made the first non-stop flight across the Atlantic. It took $16^{1}/_{2}$ hours.

▶ Today a flight from London to New York in *Concorde*, the world's fastest passenger airplane, takes only $3^{1}/_{2}$ hours.

Model T Ford cars started pouring off the factory production lines in America.

Since then, the machines that move us about have become bigger, faster and more efficient. In the olden days it would have taken a human a whole day to cover thirty miles on foot. Now we can cover the same distance in a half hour or less by road or rail. And in a whole day you can fly halfway round the world!

ENGINE POWER

The machines that have been invented to carry us and our goods from place to place include some of the most complicated ones in the world. A modern jet aircraft, an ocean liner, and a high speed train are all 'mega-machines' designed to do just one simple job – get us from A to B. Even the average family car is very complex, with thousands of parts all working together to take you a mile or a hundred miles!

Such complicated machines depend on engines or motors to make them go. Here you can see some of the 'power units' that replace the muscle power of our own legs.

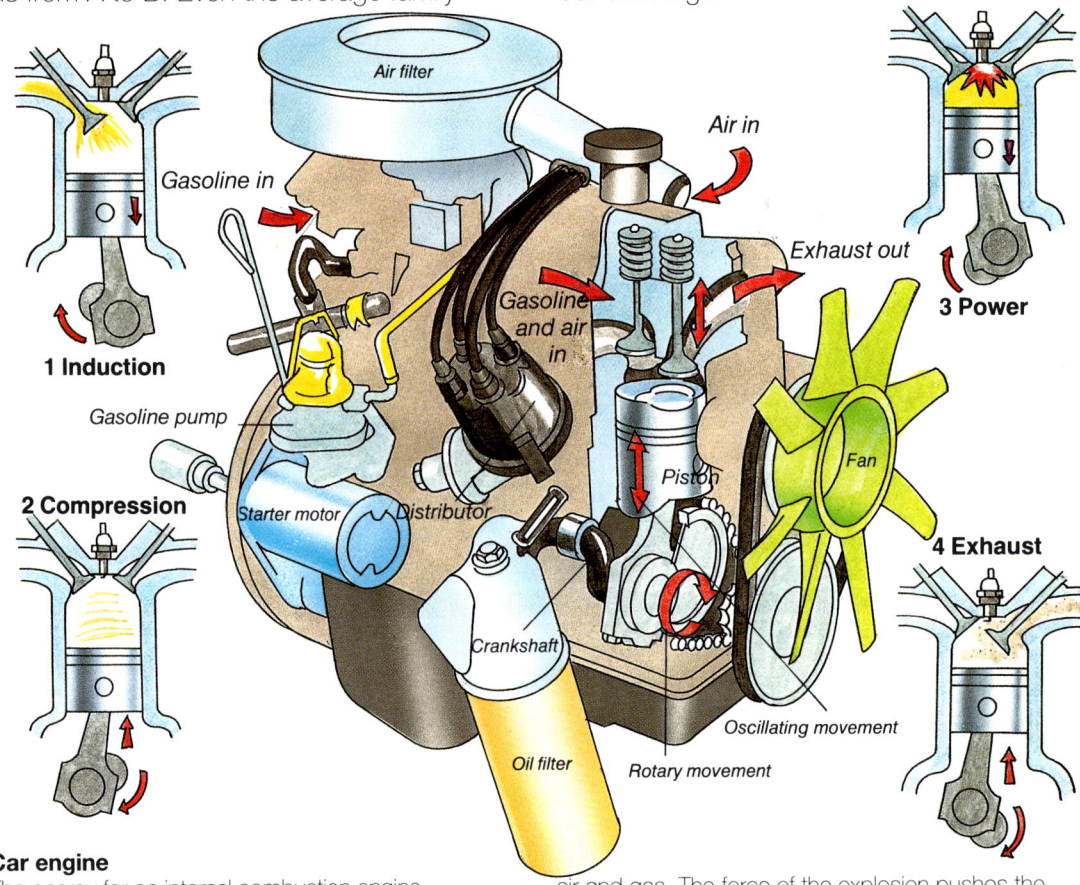

Car engine

The energy for an internal combustion engine comes from chemical bonds in the molecules of gasoline. Most car engines have four pistons and cylinders. And they work in a four-stroke cycle as follows:

1 *Induction:* Air and gasoline vapor are sucked into the space inside the cylinder as the piston goes down.
2 *Compression:* The piston then comes up and squashes the air and gas. This makes it hot and ready to explode.
3 *Power:* A spark from the spark plug ignites the air and gas. The force of the explosion pushes the piston down again.
4 *Exhaust:* Waste gases from the explosion are pushed out of the cylinder. Now the sequence is ready to start again.

The bottom of the piston is connected by a 'connecting rod' (often called a *con-rod*) to the crankshaft, where the to-and-from motion of the piston is turned into a rotary movement. This movement is then controlled in a gear box and transferred to the car's wheels via another long rod called the propellor shaft and more gears.

34

Jet engine

In a simple jet engine, air is sucked in and compressed by turbine blades. It is mixed with kerosene vapor and burns with explosive force. The hot gases rush out the back and push the engine along.

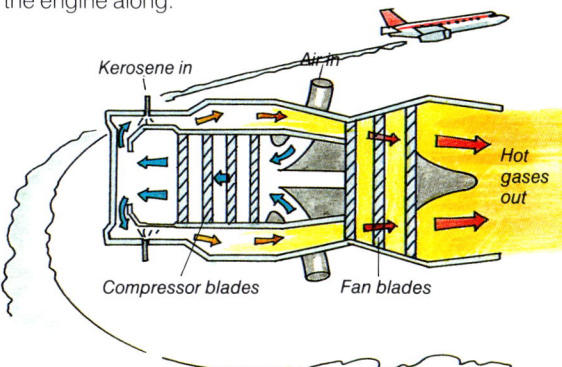

Elevator

An elevator hangs on a cable that runs over pulleys. On the cable is a counterweight as heavy as the elevator itself. The electric motor turns the pulleys to raise or lower the elevator and, because of the counterweight, has only to raise the weight of the people inside. Usually, the pulleys and cables are in a block-and-tackle arrangement to make lifting easier for the electric motor.

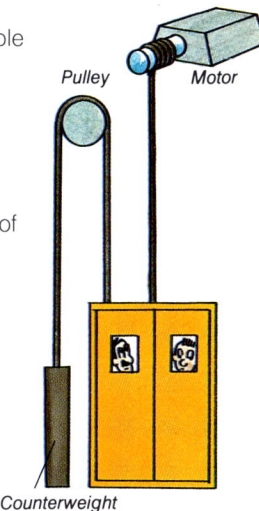

Hovercraft

To move a hovercraft, there are two sets of fans, usually driven by gas turbine engines. The lifting fans blow air into the rubber skirt of the hovercraft and lift it slightly off the ground. The propulsion fans (propellers) blow air out behind the hovercraft to push it forward.

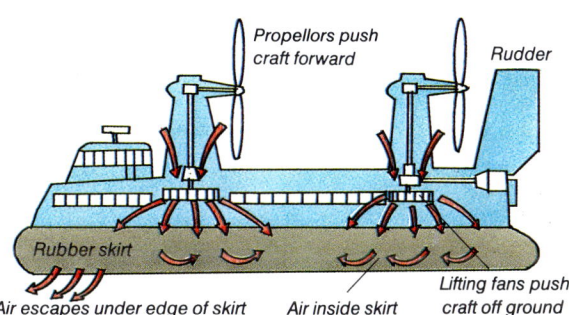

Science in action

Get in gear!

Gear wheels, as you probably know, are metal discs with teeth cut out of them. These teeth link together with the teeth from another wheel so that, when one wheel turns, the other one does too – but in the opposite direction. You have probably noticed gears like this on bicycles or inside clocks.

Although they might all look the same, gear wheels can be used in three different ways. The first way is to transfer a force from one axle to another, and so from one place to another. Gear wheels are good at doing this because of the precise way in which they join. If properly designed they will not slip or waste much energy. The second way that gears are used is to reverse the direction of a rotating force. In other words, a gear wheel that is turning clockwise will turn the wheel next to it counter-clockwise.

Finally, gears are also used to change the nature of a force, from slow and strong to fast and weak (or vice versa). This is how the gears are used on bicycles to make pedaling up steep hills a little easier!

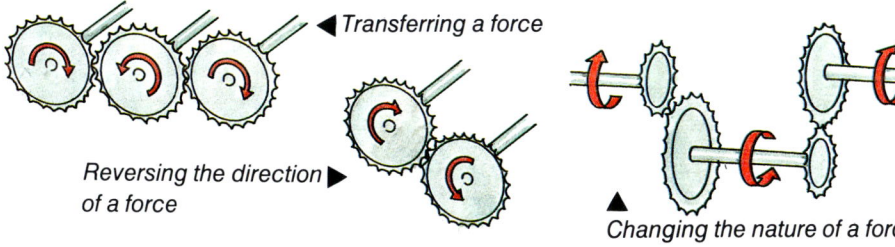

◀ Transferring a force

Reversing the direction ▶
of a force

▲
Changing the nature of a force

EXPERIMENT · EXPER

Most forms of transport these days use an engine to produce the moving force. But it would take many years of studying for you to be able to build your own proper engine. Instead, why not make a model hovercraft like the one shown opposite. Or see for yourself the idea behind jet propulsion by making a rocket like the one on this page. You can read more about engines and how they work on pages 34 and 35.

Step 1

Make a hole through the lid of the bottle which is just big enough to take the thin straw. Poke the straw through, leaving about 5½ in (14 cms) sticking up above the lid. Seal any air-holes with glue. This will be your rocket's launching pad.

Step 2

Cut the fat straw down to about 3⅛ in (8 cms) in length. Make sure that it slides over the thinner straw with ease. Then cut four paper triangles and stick them around one end of the fat straw to form the tail-end of your rocket. Seal the nose end with a piece of clay, as shown below.

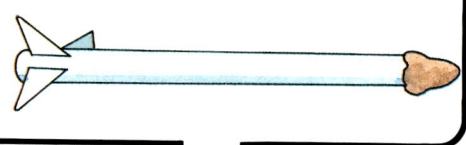

Step 3

Slide your rocket into its launching position. (The tip of the launching pad straw should stick lightly to the rocket's clay tip.) Now squeeze the bottle quickly... your rocket should shoot across the room!

As you squeeze the bottle, the air inside it becomes compressed. The result of this is that the air shoots up the only possible escape route – the thin straw – and forces your rocket forward into flight.

Experiment 4

Rocket power!

Jet engines use compressed air mixed with an explosive substance to create a strong force to move them along. Here, you can make a short-lived version using compressed air. You'll need a 'squeezable' plastic bottle with a screw-on lid, one fat and one thin straw, a sheet of paper and a lump of clay. Glue, scissors and a drill will also come in handy.

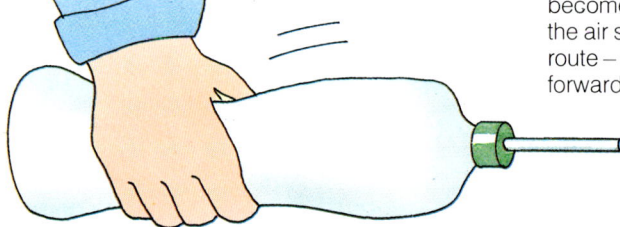

IMENT · EXPERIMENT

Experiment 5

The hovering hovercraft

All you need to make a simple hovercraft model is a light plastic food tray (like those used for fruit and vegetables in supermarkets), a small cork, a balloon, and a sheet of cardboard. Glue, scissors, a ruler, some colored pencils, and a knitting needle will also come in useful.

Step 1

Make a small hole in the middle of your tray by using a sharp pencil point. Bore a similar sized hole through the middle of your cork using the knitting needle (your parents may be able to help you with this). Then carefully line up both holes and glue the widest end of the cork to the tray. Make sure there are no air gaps.

Step 2

Using your sheet of cardboard, create a cabin for the passengers and crew like the one in the picture below. Before attaching it to the tray, use your colored pencils to draw in windows, doors, and even the people themselves on the sides of the cabin. Your hovercraft is now ready for its first voyage! Take it to a large, smooth surface – a polished floor would be ideal – along with your balloon.

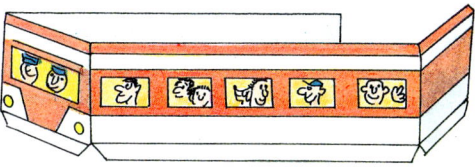

Step 3

Now, blow up your balloon. Hold the mouthpiece tightly so that the air inside cannot escape, and carefully fit it over the cork. Give the tray a gentle push and it should begin to glide away. The air from the balloon is escaping down through the cork and out from the base of the tray. As it rushes out beneath the model, it forms a cushion of air on which the hovercraft rides. In a real hovercraft this air is trapped in a 'skirt' (a rubber tube which runs around the bottom of the craft) and the forward motion is produced by propellers.

FIELD & FACTORY

Before the age of machines, most people lived in the countryside. They grew their own food and made their own clothes and other utensils. When the machines came, factories could make clothes and other items much faster and cheaper. But the machines needed looking after. So gradually people moved from the countryside into the towns and cities.

By the mid-nineteenth century, factory towns had become rather unpleasant places. Workers crowded into small houses in narrow streets, and soot and smog polluted the air. Some factory-owners did not care about their workers. Wages were low, working hours long, and many machines were dangerous to operate. Gradually however, workers managed to organize themselves, and their pay and working conditions improved.

Meanwhile, back in the countryside farmers were facing a new problem. The people in the towns and cities needed food which they couldn't grow themselves but, because so many people had moved away, the farmers had no one to help them grow the crops and raise animals. The only answer was to invent more machines to help out!

Seed drills (invented in 1702) planted seeds under the soil in neat rows; before this they were thrown onto the soil and most were eaten by birds. The threshing machine (invented in 1786) separated the useful grain of the crop from the stalks and other useless bits. The reaping machine (invented in 1826) meant that one man could cut crops twenty or thirty times faster than he could have done using the old method – a simple scythe. By the beginning of the twentieth century, the

The power of machines transformed the land. New machines meant fewer people were needed to work the land. But mines and factories needed more people, so whole towns grew up around them.

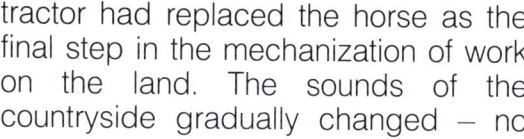

tractor had replaced the horse as the final step in the mechanization of work on the land. The sounds of the countryside gradually changed – no longer could you hear the swish of the scythe and the plodding of the cart horse. Instead, there was the chug of engines and the clank of machinery.

WORK HORSES

Thousands of years ago, in ancient Egypt, men built huge pyramids out of stone. Blocks of rock were cut and put in position by hundreds and hundreds of slaves. They worked for many years to finish their task with only a few simple machines (such as levers, rollers, ramps, ropes, and pulleys) to help them.

Nowadays, a few dozen workers could build the same pyramid in just a few months, with the help of modern machinery. Yet, although today's great machines look so advanced, they still use the basic principles of mechanics. Cranes still use pulleys, wheels, and axles. Backhoes still lever the soil out of the ground. Pneumatic drills still drive a wedge into a rock. And holes are still made by screw-shaped drills. Archimedes would no doubt be very impressed with our achievements, but he would probably still recognize his ideas at work.

Man and his animals were the work horses of yesteryear. Today, machines have taken their place. Here are a few that are used to do a lot of work for us on the land – in farming and building.

Combine harvester

This enormous contraption is really several machines 'combined' into one. First, it cuts the wheat or other crop with rotating blades. Then it threshes the wheat with a spinning cylinder that separates the grain from the stalk and chaff. It stores the grain in a large tank and unloads it via a funnel into a trailer or truck. And, finally, it binds the stalks into straw bales that fall out at the back. One combine harvester can do the work of over 100 people!

Pneumatic drill

Walk by any roadworks and you'll probably find at least one pneumatic drill at work. Even if you don't actually see it, the deafening din of drill hitting stone will tell you that it's there.

Pneumatic drills run on compressed air and can be used to break up rocks and stone. The air is pumped from a diesel- or gasoline-powered compressor along a thick flexible hose into the drill's body. Here it pushes a piston hard against the drill bit several times a second. This makes the drill hammer the rock and helps to break it up. Compressed air is a safe source of energy because there is no spark to start a fire and no electricity to give you a shock.

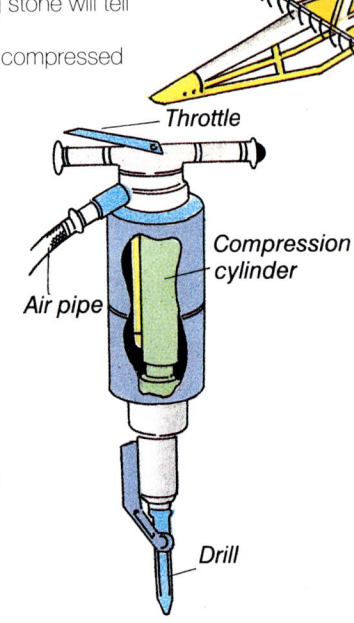

Science in action

Machines make a highway

Have you ever wondered how many machines it takes to make a highway? The answer is dozens! You can see a few of the ones involved in this panel.

With today's advanced machinery doing the work of many men, it may take only a few months to make a highway. But it can still take years and years for people to decide which route it should take!

Chain saws and loggers move any trees that are in the way of the route.

Hydraulic backhoes scoop out earth and load it into trucks or earth movers. They dig away hills, fill in valleys and make trenches for drains.

Bulldozers distribute the earth evenly and level the ground.

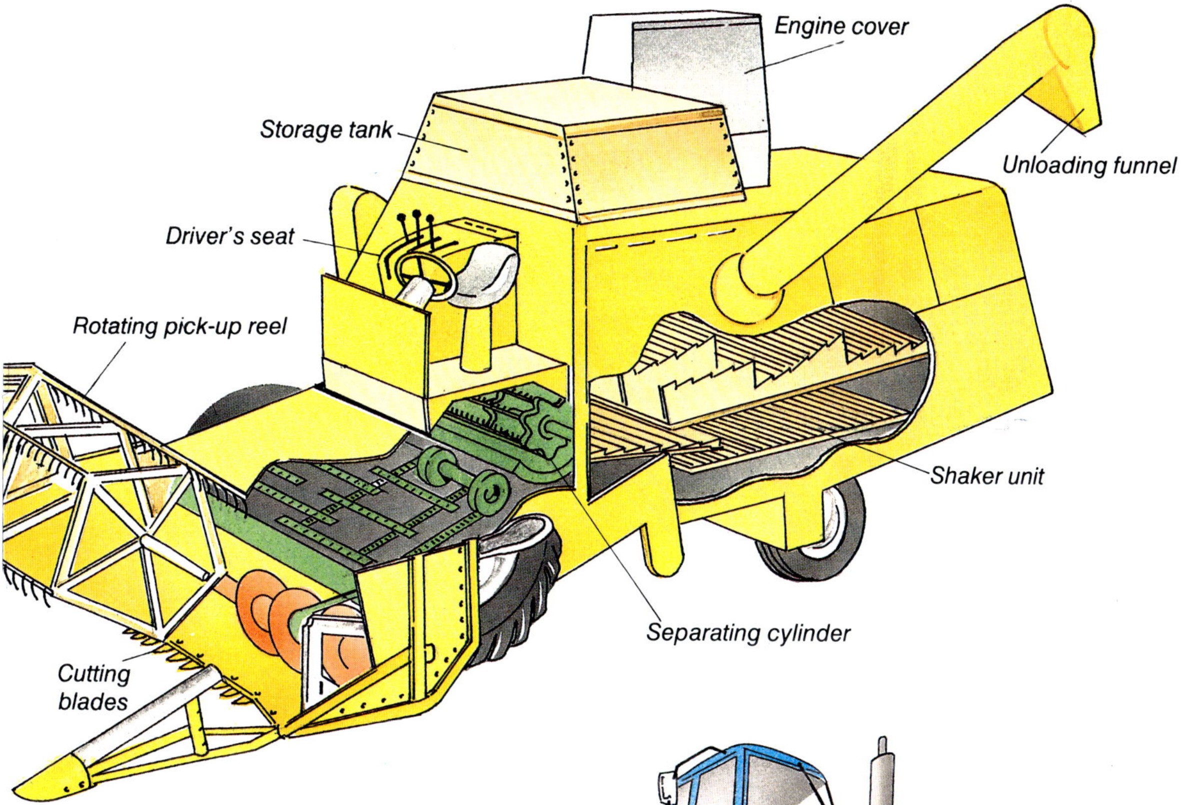

Engine cover

Storage tank

Driver's seat

Rotating pick-up reel

Unloading funnel

Shaker unit

Separating cylinder

Cutting blades

Tractor
Tractors are designed to pull all sorts of machinery, from plows to hay-turners. They are usually powered by diesel engine and have large rear wheels to give them a good grip in mud or soft earth. Besides turning the wheels, a tractor's engine can be disconnected and used to drive other machines such as a hydraulic digger or a water pump.

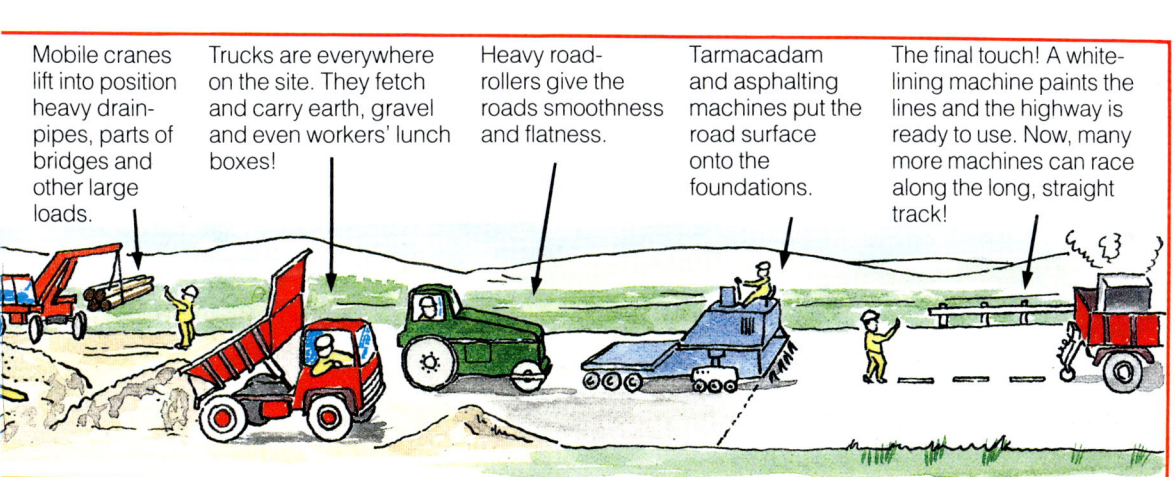

Mobile cranes lift into position heavy drain-pipes, parts of bridges and other large loads.

Trucks are everywhere on the site. They fetch and carry earth, gravel and even workers' lunch boxes!

Heavy road-rollers give the roads smoothness and flatness.

Tarmacadam and asphalting machines put the road surface onto the foundations.

The final touch! A white-lining machine paints the lines and the highway is ready to use. Now, many more machines can race along the long, straight track!

41

THINGS TO REMEMBER

What the words mean....

As a young scientist, you will find words that are new and confusing in this book. Or words that are familiar to you, but take on a more precise meaning when used scientifically. Here are some explanations of such words. Hopefully, they will help you to understand more fully the principles of mechanics.

BLOCK AND TACKLE A series of ropes and pulleys used for lifting and towing heavy objects.

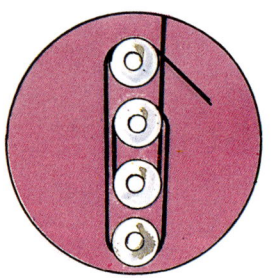

EFFICIENCY The amount of energy put into a machine that is actually turned into useful work. It is usually written as a percentage.

ENERGY The capacity or ability to do work. Energy is measured in joules.

ENGINE A complex machine that uses energy to produce movement for a certain job – generally, to work another machine.

ENGINEER Someone who designs, builds or maintains machines.

FORCE The 'push' that makes an object move, or changes its speed or direction. It is measured in Newtons.

FRICTION The resistance encountered when two objects rub together.

FULCRUM The point at which a lever pivots.

GEARWHEEL A wheel with a toothed edge that meshes with another gearwheel or the holes in a chain.

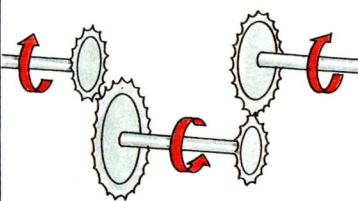

GRAVITY The natural attraction of one object to another but, particularly, of all objects to the Earth.

HORSEPOWER A unit of power expressing rate of work. It is not a metric unit but is still used for many machines such as cars and boats.

INCLINED PLANE A simple machine, consisting of a slope or ramp, which can be used to make lifting heavy objects easier.

INDUSTRIAL REVOLUTION The period, starting around 1750 and lasting about 100 years, when steam and other engines were invented, factories were built, and machines became far more numerous and complicated.

KINETIC ENERGY The energy something possesses because of its movement, such as flowing water or a spinning flywheel.

LEVER A simple machine consisting of a rigid rod or pole that pivots at the fulcrum.

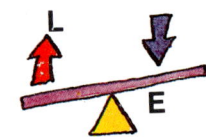

LINEAR MOVEMENT Movement in a straight line.

42

MECHANIC Someone who understands machines and movement, or who maintains complicated machines such as cars or trains.

MECHANICS The science of machines and movement.

NEWTON A unit of force that gives an object weighing one kilogram an acceleration of one meter per second every second.

OSCILLATING MOVEMENT Movement in a to-and-fro or backwards-and-forwards manner.

POTENTIAL ENERGY The energy something possesses because of its position, such as a car at the top of a hill, or a stretched piece of elastic.

POWER The rate at which work is done. It is measured in horsepower or watts.

PULLEY A simple machine made up of a wheel with a grooved rim in which runs a cable or rope.

RESISTANCE A force that 'steals' energy from moving things.

ROTARY MOVEMENT Movement in a round-and-round manner.

SCREW A simple machine consisting of an inclined plane or wedge wrapped in spiral fashion around a central rod or axle.

WATT A unit of power, expressing rate of work.

WEDGE A simple machine consisting of two inclined planes, back-to-back.

WHEEL AND AXLE A simple machine made up of a disc shape that acts as a 'continuous lever', rotating about its center on an axle.

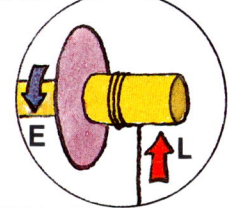

WORK The result of a force moving an object. Like energy, it is measured in joules.

EXPERIMENT AND PROJECT INDEX

A hundred machines? 31
Everyday machines 30
Fighting friction 14
Making a steam turbine 25
Newton's Cradle 16
Rocket Power! 36
Supper by sunlight! 24
The hovering hovercraft 37

43